Self-Harming and Suicide: searching for answers

An exploration by

The SPEAK Project, Short Strand

compiled by

Michael Hall

ISLAND (73) PAMPHLETS

Published August 2005 by Island Publications
132 Serpentine Road, Newtownabbey, Co Antrim BT36 7JQ

mikeohall@hotmail.com

ISBN 1 899510 65 6

Farset Community Think Tanks Project is funded by:

The EU Special Support Programme for Peace and Reconciliation
administered through the **Northern Ireland Community Relations Council**

with the assistance, for this pamphlet, of **The Ireland Funds**

On behalf of the SPEAK Project (Strand Parents Educators And Kids) I would like to thank number of people and funders whose support made the project possible:

Bernie Black, who pushed and assisted our work on behalf of Short Strand Community Foru

Paul McCrory, whose professionalism as a youth leader gave the project guidance

South & East Belfast Health and Social Care Group, without whose funding the project could never have developed

Groundwork, **EBCHIP**, **Bytes**, **Short Strand Youth Victims Project**, and **Joe Hinds**

And last, but certainly not least, those people – young and not so young – who took part and gave their full support to the project.

Sean Montgomery

Because of the personal nature of the contributions it was decided not to list the participants' names

Printed by Regency Press, Belfast

Introduction

ıe current increase in incidents of self-harming and suicide, especially among ›ung people, has engendered vociferous demands for an injection of resources to those communities identified as being at greatest risk, although it is becoming ɜar that *every* community is vulnerable, and that *any* family could easily be e next to be visited by tragedy.

The resources called for range from the establishment of locally-based awareness ogrammes to the provision of adequate professional medical and counselling rvices. But, while all of these are vital, there is *no greater resource* than the rsonal experience of those who have been most closely affected. And it is ith remarkable openness and courage that a number of young people and rents – associated with the SPEAK Project based in Short Strand, East Belfast proved willing to describe their personal experiences and share their thoughts this pamphlet, in the hope that what they have to say might be of help to hers confronting similar situations.

To those who feel helpless in the face of circumstances over which they seem have little or no control, the young people and parents of the SPEAK project ve a straightforward message: the simple act of sharing our pain and our oblems with others can be the first step on the long road to recovery.

Michael Hall, *Farset Community Think Tanks Project*

Sean Montgomery, *Short Strand Community Centre*

Self-Harming and Suicide: searching for answers

Creating a support group

The work currently being done in Short Strand on the issues of self-harmi and suicide is centred around the SPEAK project, involving young people a parents. Sean Montgomery, community development worker, and Paul McCro youth worker, have been instrumental in initiating and sustaining this projec

> The SPEAK project is a fairly new programme, it started within the last year. And what we have tried to do is to establish a forum for young people who have self-harmed or had thoughts of suicide – or even attempted suicide. We wanted to create an environment where those young people can feel secure, where they can share their personal experiences and become more aware of all the different issues that are impacting upon their lives.
>
> The idea was that the programme would, first of all, provide an opportunity for young people to come together and feel they have a voice, both individually and as a group. The hope was that, having heard each other's experiences, they could begin to accept that each one of them was not on their own, that it wasn't just them – or somebody related to them – who was self-harming or contemplating suicide, but that it's a growing issue in the wider community, for many people. The next stage then would be to provide different bits of training to the group, not only to help them as individuals but to see if they in turn could assist others. And, as part of that, a drama project was put together, which not only served to get a 'message' across to other young people out there, but, through their actual participation in it, allowed each member of the group to develop on a personal level and become much more aware of where they are. Drama is a good tool for doing that.
>
> In the drama, and also in the role-playing which formed part of the training, you could see that some of the scenarios the young people were acting out had actually occurred in their own lives. Now, we obviously made sure that at any stage they could draw back from things; we didn't want them to feel vulnerable. But generally they seemed to benefit tremendously from it, and tackling the issues as a group also served to reinforce to them that there *is* support there if they want it, they needn't go through things on their own.
>
> The issues of self-harming and suicide throw up two almost contradictory misperceptions. On the one hand, the individual who is self-harming, or having suicidal thoughts, often thinks that this is only happening to them, with the result that they can feel very isolated. And these individuals, whether

they be young people or adults, need to be made aware that they are *not* alone and that help is available. At the same time, you have a situation where many families who haven't been affected by these issues think it only happens to other people, it could never happen to anyone in *their* family. The community must be made aware that it can happen in *any* family, and be assisted to look out for tell-tale signs in their own children.

Such misperceptions are changing, however. In the last couple of years the high incidence of suicide among young people has really hit home to communities everywhere, and I think more and more people now accept that it's not just something that happens to other people's children.

The training the young people did was intensive. We had workshops, some of which involved both young people and adults in putting together a 'safe plan' which could be used to talk someone away from self-harming or suicidal thoughts. But the thing I found most valuable was that it created an atmosphere where people were being very open and honest. Everybody was allowed the space to participate, not only to hear the message being delivered by the training course, but, more importantly, to share their own experiences and to actively listen to the experiences of others. It was also positive to hear from those who had some hands-on experience of the problem, or had useful information to share about the issues and how to confront them.

he workers themselves made sure that the support offered was not restricted lely to the training sessions, as Paul noted:

We put in place a lot of safety nets. I would try to take a lot of the hassle out of the young people's lives – for example, in terms of dealing with their parents or others, who might be angry when the young people are disruptive. And with each young person who I might work with I would often end any one-to-one discussion with a 'debriefing' session where I would make sure they knew where they had got to, and what the issues had been, as well as make sure that there weren't unresolved matters still worrying them.

In areas like Short Strand you can never 'step out' of your work. Once you finish your stint in the youth club or the community centre and go round to the pub for a beer – or maybe you're standing on the street corner – people are continually discussing different problems and issues. To be involved in this type of work has to be a labour of love in a sense. But you can see successes. Many of the young people who participated in activities with us – and I'm personally going back three or four years – are now actively helping out in terms of youth and community work.

More people out there know that there are people like ourselves within the community who have undertaken a bit of training in terms of self-harming and suicide. Now, we're not in any way claiming to be full-blown counsellors, it's more the case that we have a 'first-aid' type of awareness when it comes to self-harming and suicide. But the most important thing is the fact that the young people have someone to talk to.

In terms of confronting the problem, what did the workers think society response should be, and what should statutory agencies be doing?

> I think the response must operate at several levels, and I think everybody has a role to play. In the first instance people like ourselves, who are working on the ground and have first-hand experience of what's going on – in terms of the issues in young people's lives – can be the first 'port of call', and I don't think you can replace that. But certainly, in terms of delivering quality follow-up help, I think professional back-up has to be available. In the immediate and short term it's a case of creating somewhere safe for young people – and others – to come to and talk about the issues which affect them. But at the same time having resource options available where you can say to someone who is really going through a difficult time: 'Look, I'd like to suggest you go and see so-and-so.'

> Yes, I think we all need to work together. We need to know that there are professionals within the statutory agencies and medical profession who can assist with individual cases. In turn, the professionals need to know that we are a community resource which can equally assist those individuals, but in a different way. We all really need to be working together.

> I don't think most people on the ground can see any real, tangible statutory response to the whole issue, other than the fact that the agenda has certainly moved on – and you can tell that from all the media attention it gets. However, there still remains this notion that if only sufficient money was made available that would be the end of the problem, and there is much frustration and anger out there that these resources are not readily available. But, of course, it's never as simple as that. For a start nobody can tell for sure where to direct those resources best, and we won't know that until we fully understand the root causes. Nevertheless, I think the statutory agencies need to be playing a more active role, and not just talking about the issues. There needs to be a process in place where people on the ground like ourselves who can identify likely problems – or who are often the first to be approached by individuals seeking help – can be assured that when we feel the help we can offer has to move on to another level then the necessary resources are in place and functioning efficiently. I mean, sometimes we refer what we would consider 'urgent' cases to professionals and the individual is told they'll be sent out an appointment in a few weeks' time, or even months in some cases.

> Also, it's the whole thing about proper communication, especially when several agencies are involved. Some of the kids I work with tell me they are involved with Probation, or Social Services, and you're saying to yourself: this is crazy, each of us is working in a vacuum here. We should have some type of forum where we can work together on general issues, and another type of forum where – with proper safeguards as to confidentiality – agencies can work together to help particular individuals.

Did the workers feel that the rise in incidents of suicide was related in any way to the decades of political turmoil and violence?

There is a suggestion that the Troubles has played some role in it. But I don't think we are in a position to narrow it down and say it's because of this or that – there's a whole raft of reasons as to why it happens. A lot more work needs to be put into determining the root causes. I think part of it is that society has become more selfish, more concerned with 'keeping up with the Joneses', and people are far less respectful to one another. And young people are under terrible pressure to have the latest gear, to always do well, to join their peers in the whole drug and alcohol scene – there's a whole lot of demands and expectations made on kids nowadays. And although young people these days have more money and possessions than previous generations, they don't seem to know the value of things, and often feel they need more. And when they see their parents competing for possessions they think it's natural to want to do the same.

And then, of course, there's all the social and economic issues which impact on our communities: the lack of job opportunities, the long-term unemployment, the loss of self-esteem and all the other problems.

nd what were their hopes for this pamphlet?

We just want to initiate a debate. There are no real answers as yet, but at least we can let people – whether young people or their parents – share their personal experiences, in the hope that other troubled young people or their parents who read this pamphlet will realise that they are not alone and that there is support available. But, basically, if we can get more people talking about the issues that'll be great, and people can take it on from there.

The young people

he young people (aged between 15 and 25) undertook their own series of scussions. They spoke first about the genesis of the project.

There was a spate of suicides all over Belfast, and there was groups being set up, like PIPS in Ardoyne, and others in West Belfast. And because there were a couple of young people self-harming around here, or who had tried to commit suicide and things like that, some people had the idea of getting a support group in Short Strand going too.

We began with a wee group through Groundwork and then the SPEAK project was started about a year ago.

Although the media focus has mostly been on North Belfast, there have been a lot of young people round here who have self-harmed. My cousin committed suicide and he lived round here. There must be others who have either thought of or attempted to kill themselves, but who either haven't told anyone or their family has kept it quiet. So it was about setting up a support group, to try and help young people who might be contemplating it, trying to get the warnings out and stuff like that.

Yes, many young people would feel embarrassed if they had self-harmed or had thought about suicide, so they wouldn't go around telling a load of people. My mate attempted suicide, but other than in our circle of friends you wouldn't have knew. He tried to overdose, and then felt ashamed about it afterwards.

A friend of mine overdosed too, but she didn't take enough, and she brought herself to hospital.

I know a few young people who were self-harming but managed to hide it from their families – cutting their arms, or even their back, where it couldn't be seen under their jumpers... stuff like that.

But if they *don't* tell people, and don't get the help or the support they need, then the next time it might be too late. That's why we wanted this wee support group to be there.

That wee boy in Ardoyne killed himself on St. Valentine's Day and on the day of his funeral his best friend says to his mother: 'Give me some money to buy a packet of fags, I'm going to the shop.' And he went out and climbed up the scaffolding of the church and hung himself.

Aye, the day before the funeral, when he was leaning into his friend's coffin, he was overheard saying: 'You were meant to wait on me, we were supposed to do this together.' And his family talked and talked to him and everything, but it didn't stop him. I think the two of them must have planned it.

I know another person who hung herself too. She was older, she had three kids and it was her wee girl, only 13, who went in and found her.

My uncle had to kick down a door one day because this man was thought to have committed suicide. The man's wife was standing behind my uncle and once he got into the house your man was hanging there at the top of the stairs. His wife just completely flipped.

That's the way a friend of mine was on finding his bother. His brother was standing talking to him and then he said 'I'll be back in a minute'. But when he didn't came back my friend went round and found the door locked and knew something was wrong. And he started banging the door and got his mummy out of bed and when he ran upstairs he saw the loft door open. And when he got into the loft he found that his brother had hung himself. My friend actually put his foot through the ceiling trying to grab his brother down. I think his brother killed himself 'cause he couldn't get any work.

What did they think drove young people to self-harm or suicidal thoughts?

Trying to escape problems: family problems, debt problems.

There's a lot of people have not been able to get jobs, or proper training opportunities to be able to get jobs. Also, in many areas there's not enough for young people to do.

Well, some people say it's because of the lack of jobs, or the fact that there's nothing to do. But then other people say there are no obvious reasons at all. I know of a girl who hung herself some years ago, and to this day her family still can't understand the reason why she did it.

I agree. I don't know if you can ever understand the true reasons why it happens. I know of somebody who committed suicide a few months ago and he had a half-decent wee job going. He had a child as well, but just for some reason he killed himself.

Everybody is different, but I suppose there are some risk areas. For a start, in an area like this, as has already been said, there's not many activities for young people to do. If they're lucky they might get onto a local football team, but generally there aren't a lot of facilities and stuff for young people, so they're turning to drinking and drugs. Many young people today find that peer pressure forces them into taking drugs and stuff like that there. And that doesn't help. Boredom and all comes into it, and sometimes that can lead on to thoughts of suicide. That's just some of the things we found which might lead to it.

I think it's our age group too. Pensioners have their wee do's all the time, and the younger kids have their youth clubs and get going away on trips. But there's nothing for my age group. I'm 24, and all I can do is go and get drunk or take drugs. There's nothing really for people my age to do.

Depression is another reason. And family problems.

Bullying is another: people giving you a hard time at school.

But sometimes it's people who look really happy who commit suicide – happy and outgoing, the ones you would least expect.

Aye, the quiet ones probably keep it bottled in until one day they're just ready to burst.

People who seem very outgoing. That's the way it was for me. See right until I was 18, until I had a nervous breakdown, I was always running about having a bit of craic, slegging everybody, drinking. And then one day I couldn't even walk outside the door, my bangers [nerves] were away, and I couldn't cope with anything. Everything just shut down like that. I didn't want to live. That's how quick it turns.

Exam stress is another.

Aye. I think GCSEs are a lot of pressure and all the coursework is fired onto you at the same time of the year.

Anyway, most people round here even with GCSEs are going to end up in Burger King or somewhere like that. The type of area we come from puts employers off. They see you as a hood, just because of the area.

One person I knew who killed himself had tried it loads of times before; almost every week he was in hospital for either taking an overdose or slashing his wrists.

Some of the suicides were the result of run-ins with the paramilitaries. Some paramilitaries go around acting like hard men, and they try to scare young people. I know one wee boy who was really afraid to go outside his house.

One wee lad who committed suicide was getting bate every second week by the paramilitaries.

But I don't think that's the reason for most young people feeling suicidal; there's other reasons. Such as their parents' lack of interest. Many parents don't take much interest in their kids.

Parents wouldn't really sit you down and say: 'What's the matter, are you all right, what's the craic?' They wouldn't do that.

That's true. There are a lot of young people whose parents are too busy, or they don't care, or they have other family issues to attend to. Or they *do* care but they just don't realise things are that bad.

They should watch out for things like erratic behaviour, or mood swings, and locking yourself in your room.

My ma got the doctor for me, because I just used to go home and go to bed after school!

Same with my family. I took a turn and they took me straight away to the doctor's. But I was glad they did.

But, really, there is no list of 'warning signs' you can point to. Everyone is different. And some of the things we might point to as warning signs – like lying on in bed all day, or always fighting with their wee brothers, and things like that – are just a normal part of growing up for many young people.

I think the problem nowadays is that both boys and girls are all growing up too quickly. They're getting into sex, drink and drugs, and all that lark, much younger than young people used to, and they wouldn't be able to talk to their parents as easy.

And they're probably too embarrassed to even talk to their mates.

They might *try* to talk to their mates, but many of their mates might not be good listeners; they will probably just laugh, and that will put more pressure on them.

There's been a lot of mad stuff going around, glamorising suicide. Like that 'Virgin Suicides' film. Then you had the Columbine school shootings in America, and people like Marlyn Manson. There's even internet groups for potential suicides now.

I think some young people think suicide is an easy way out for them. They say to themselves: 'What's here for me?' And if they don't find any purpose in life they think it's an easy option.

I think it's largely because there's nothing to do, you have more time to think and it just drives you mad. My friend tried to kill herself and when I asked her why she did it she said: 'I just have too much time to think; just sitting on my own I'd be thinking about the stupidest wee things. But sometimes these thoughts make me ask myself: why am I here? what's the point in life? is there any point in going through all this? I could just end it here and now and get it over and done with.'

I don't think we can say just what causes suicide, because you're not in anybody's mind who has committed suicide. You can't say: 'Yes, this is why they did it.' Everyone obviously has an opinion on why, but that's all it is, an opinion, and until you're in that situation you can't say: 'This is the reason why they did that.'

Sometimes people don't really know what they're doing, or whether they really want to go ahead with it. A friend of my sister was a really quiet person, with a wife and kids and all. But yet he hung himself. She said you wouldn't have thought that he wanted to do something like that. And whenever he was lying in the coffin you could see the scratch marks down his neck, 'cause he must have been trying to get the rope off again.

Everybody has different reasons for committing suicide, and there's probably some reasons we wouldn't have expected.

Aye, they might have something worrying them that wouldn't worry us, but they might be experiencing it a hundred times worse than we do.

I think every young person these days goes through a phase where they might think about suicide.

I did. It scared me at the time, but luckily it passed.

People sometimes confuse a cry for help with somebody just seeking attention. I did my wrists once, and that wasn't for attention. I was on medication for depression. One time I was feeling really down, and I was sitting there eating. I was using a steak knife and suddenly I felt this urge to go like that there across my wrists. Although as soon as I did it I ran upstairs roaring and crying. My ma and da were in bed but they jumped up and freaked out. But I could have just sat there and kept cutting myself.

There's probably far more people who come close to attempting suicide than we ever hear about. That's why there should be a wee drop-in centre, so that those people can come in and talk to someone.

It's hard to say really personal things to your friends. I still wouldn't say something like that even to my closest friend.

But friends *can* help you. I once said to my best friend that I was feeling suicidal and he said 'Come-on, you'll be alright.' And he sat and talked and sort of reassured me, and after that I was alright again. I didn't try to harm myself but I was at a stage where I was constantly crying and feeling really down. But just being able to talk to him helped.

Sometimes you don't feel like telling your parents in case they overreact. If I said anything to my ma – like that I was feeling depressed or something – she would probably take it too seriously and say: 'Hey, you need psychiatric help!' or something. And you don't really want to go through all that there.

When my friend's brother killed himself his mother took it really bad. She just takes tablets all the time, and she looks terrible. It just kills my mate; he hates seeing his ma like that, he even hates going into the living room because she is just so doped up.

And when your ma is doped up like that it's not your ma really, it's somebody else. It's just somebody sitting there depressed, spaced out.

And when she's like that she won't be there for her other children – they won't have someone to talk to if they have things worrying them.

One of the issues which did seem to raise deep concerns among the youn people was the 'drug scene' which now pervades more and more communitie and with such detrimental impact.

I think that drugs is a major cause of many problems, and that includes suicide, because with some of these drugs they're taking now they feel as if they are God, they're invincible. Cocaine is widely got round here as much as cannabis, which didn't happen ten years ago. And also it's more socially acceptable now for kids to take cannabis; people turn a blind eye to it. What they don't realise is that they start off with cannabis when they're maybe 12 or 13 years old, and then when they get to 15 or 16 it's not good enough for them, so they take 'E'-tabs, and then it might progress right up to cocaine.

Me personally, that's the way I started off. I started off smoking cannabis and then I started taking 'E's, and that led to me to having a nervous breakdown. And I did start to harm myself and I even contemplated committing suicide. So I think a lot of that there would be true.

I'm not so sure. My friend in Ardoyne who killed himself never took drugs. We don't want parents reading this and thinking that the reason their child harmed themselves or committed suicide was because they were on drugs. It might have been nothing to do with drugs. As we said earlier, there's a whole lot of other possible reasons.

But the whole drugs issue is still a major problem facing young people today.

Peer pressure can make it worse. Your mates can be going 'Take it, take it, you'll be alright.'

You take 'E's and you're up all night.

I think drugs, for some people, can bring out their deepest fears, things they have hidden way back in their minds, and which nobody else knows about. *They* know it but they never tell anybody. And with alcohol the hangover wears away after a day but with drugs the downer you get can last for a week.

And the situation is only going to get worse. There's even young parents 18 or 20 now taking drugs, having people round to their house taking drugs while their kids are sitting there.

And for those who have no jobs it's also easier to make money by dealing drugs.

But that's like people going on the game, hitting the Albert Clock for a weekend. People think: I could make as much in one night as I could in two weeks. A girl across the street from me went and did that. But she has a baby now and she never did it again. I think it's also because there's nothing else to do. That's what my mate says: 'I really need a job cause I have too much time to think, and that's what is triggering me.'

The drugs issue *is* important but it is only one aspect.

The young people noted that the willingness to take drugs was only one sign of major changes which have taken place in social behaviour, especially among young people.

There's other big changes as well. I'm 25 and even I can see the difference in young people, in people's attitudes towards life in general, towards society, their community – there's just no respect there. When I was 15 you didn't stand around the street corner, you did everything discretely. But now it's all in your face; the young people say: 'We don't care, we'll do what we want!' There's no respect for any voices of authority. And it's the same with some of the parents.

That's true, years ago you did things discretely. We would have taken a carry-out over to the Walkway, but it would have been hidden in a rucksack, or you had your bottle of cider hid in your coat so nobody could see it. It would have been different in the summer, for there might have been a festival going on, and you would have seen people sneak about drinking because everybody else was. But things like that has died out now. There's no festival any more, probably *because* there's too much of a drink and drug culture around here. The drinkers would ruin it, they would cause too much trouble. At the festival there used to be something for the kids and everybody else, but because of the troublemakers now there's nothing.

I think another problem is that in areas like this there is no respect for the police, and that's largely because of all the stuff they have been involved in against the Nationalist community. You need to have a policing service that you can respect. But it's not just the police that young people don't have respect for. When I was younger it would have been members of the Irish Republican movement moving you on, but these days kids don't seem to listen to them either. Before, you would have done what they told you, 'cause if you didn't they would have brought you round to see your ma and da.

Areas can be really different. I know that in some areas if the IRA approach young people they will listen to them and do what they say. But in other areas even when the IRA come along the young people tell them to 'fuck off!'

It's like that in Poleglass.

I seen it in Divis as well. People set up a Community Watch one time in Divis because the young people had no respect for anyone: they were abusing pensioners, they just more or less took over the area and were joy-riding and driving at people's houses, it was pandemonium.

See the likes of the Markets and Short Strand, when I was growing up, you wouldn't have back-chatted adults, you wouldn't have said a filthy or bad word to them – but see now? There's young people whose parents allow them to say or get up to anything they want to. Nobody checks them, not even their parents, so they just get worse.

I firmly believe that some parents are part of the problem. They'll say: 'Oh, my John wouldn't do nothing like that there, he wouldn't do that.' The adults are becoming the liars too. I remember if somebody had've brought me round to my da for doing something he'd have slapped me in front of them. But now the parents stand there and argue with you. If a kid breaks a window and is brought round to his ma or da they say: 'What makes you so sure it was my child!'

And not only that – the child will probably say: 'Da, this man hit me a dig in the head.' And then before you know it a fight starts up!

These days many young people involved in anti-social behaviour – and their parents – try to make it seem as if *they* are the victims.

However, despite these different problems – the insidious nature of the curren drug culture, the growing lack of respect for people and property among som sections of the community, and the fact that the reasons behind self-harm o suicide are complex – what did the young people think could be done to counter the rise of self-destructive incidents?

> I don't think the health service has proper resources, or they're not putting enough resources into those communities most affected. If you want to see a counsellor they maybe have a ten-minute slot for you once every three months.
>
> I think it's far better if you can go to somebody who knows the problem from living it.
>
> Yes, like a self-help group.
>
> When we finish this course, I'm hoping to go on myself and be able to help other people. Because I feel I've kinda been there and seen it.
>
> There's not enough resources being put into working-class areas.
>
> I think each local area should have a wee drop-in centre, where you can just call in and speak to someone. Not necessarily a trained counsellor, just someone people trust who they can talk to about drugs and things like that.
>
> There's occupational therapy for people but the nearest one for most people around here is on the Ravenhill Road. There's handicapped people have to go in there too, wheelchair bound and all that there, and then there's people with depression and all, but the place is too small for all of them.
>
> If somebody thinks you're a wee bit mad, it's straight into Purdysburn.
>
> No, you're not. Only in really extreme cases do you get put into Purdysburn – or Knockbracken as it is called now – it's only if you are going to harm yourself or others.
>
> But people are still afraid that's what might happen if they tell a doctor or some other professional that they're depressed or feeling suicidal. That's why you should have wee drop-in centres with people there you feel you can talk to, like community workers or youth workers.
>
> You'd imagine that schools should be a place where you could ask for help, but I think young people are more comfortable talking to a mentor or a youth leader rather than to a school teacher.
>
> If there was somebody in the school who you were supposed to go to if you had problems the other children would see you going into their room, and say: 'Oh, look, she's going for counselling!' So you wouldn't go to them.
>
> Aye, I don't think I would go and talk to a teacher or a counsellor. I would prefer to go and talk to somebody outside school. A mentor perhaps.
>
> Anyway, in school I never learned anything about real life, it was all focused on education and exams. You maybe learned in religion about abortion and

euthanasia and things like that, but you were just being told the Catholic Church's line on these things; there was nothing about the issues that would have affected your everyday life.

Well, where I went to school on the Crumlin Road they got a fella out to talk about suicide.

Yes, I think they should have somebody going round the schools. There was a guy once came round and talked about his brother having a drink problem.

We're doing a thing in school about personal development: sexual maturity and things like that. So some schools are different.

Talking about school I think more integrated education would help.

In terms of self-harming or suicide? How would it?

'Cause sometimes I feel trapped in Short Strand; you're afraid to go outside the area. And I know a lot of young people around here feel the same way. The only place we can go to is into town, and even then you're still worried about being attacked coming back over the bridge. So the more contacts you have with young people outside your own area the better. There'd be more options of things to do, and I think that would lift a lot of the pressures on some young people.

How did the group feel their project was progressing?

The drama we all did was very successful. It was as much targeted towards parents, encouraging them to talk to their children about different issues, like drugs and suicide. And in the drama we tried to act out things they should look out for. Like drinking, fighting, coming home late at night. And things they mightn't know was going on, like underage sex, joy-riding, robbing people...

There was a wee discussion after it.

It went very well. It was even shocking to a lot of young people who came along, because at the end of the play the wee girl in the play hangs herself, and the audience didn't realise it might have led to that... She had started off by having a carry-out at the corner and that led to other things. I think many parents are ignorant of the way one thing can lead to another. And, as we were saying earlier, underage drinking has become more socially acceptable now. The kids say: 'Don't worry, we're only having a few tins of beer', but really they're getting full and causing havoc.

The drama had been done before in Ardoyne and different places.

We have to get the schools and the parents to take a greater interest in what's happening to young people, for if they don't then the problems will just build up.

Our project is an attempt to make people aware of the issues. Or even better, to get them to join in. Pens and things have been given out with phone numbers on them.

Aye, because even wee simple things help. Like setting up help-lines. There's not enough Freephone helplines.

After we complete the training we will see if we want to run a drop-in centre. But we need funding, we need an office to work from.

I would like to get qualifications to become a counsellor to help others.

One of the young people ended one of the discussions with a comment which spoke volumes:

We could talk here all night, couldn't we? It's always adults who do the talking, never the young people.

The parents

Some of the parents, meeting separately, spoke of their own personal experiences.

I had a young nephew who took his own life when he was 15. His mother had left him at home that evening – she was going to a hospital appointment – and he was due to start work an hour or so later. And she had left his clean clothes out and he seemed in the best of form. But when she came home from hospital it was to find that he had hung himself in the garage. Not only was it devastating to the whole family but it was a terrible shock to everyone. I remember getting all my kids together round the table that night and saying to them: 'Look, there's nothing bad that you can do, nothing terrible that you could tell me that I probably haven't heard before, so never be afraid to come and tell me or your mother if you have done something you feel really worried about.' I was scared that one of my own kids could find themselves in trouble and be afraid to come and tell us what they were going through.

My youngest daughter – she's almost 20 now – has been a disturbed child all her life. She was referred to a child psychologist from she was seven years of age, and nobody could find out the reasons behind her disturbed behaviour, both at home and in school. In school, instead of letting her disrupt the rest of the class the teacher just made her sit beside him, and this went on for years. As she grew into a teenager she was bullied at school and everything else, even though she was a big girl. She got very disruptive at home, and just would not take part in anything – you know, family discussions or anything at all. My other children would have sat down and talked about things, even about decorating the house. But if you had asked her 'What colour will we paint it?' she'd reply: 'I don't care. Paint it black.' She just became totally alien to the family. Her sister had died of an illness, then her mother died too, and about a fortnight after her mother's death she disappeared for about three days: we couldn't find her anywhere, I had everybody out looking for her. She was almost 18 then so the police didn't take it too seriously. They told us that teenagers often go away to a party and then stay with friends... you know, the usual. But she had never done anything like that before. She eventually came home, and gave four or five different explanations as to where she was. Then, after a few more months she really went out of control. She demanded to go out whenever she wanted to, and would not do anything at home; did no housework, wouldn't even clean her own room. She left home once more and came back again, but I put her out this time. She went and stayed with one of her aunts and told lies that I was always fighting with her, and wouldn't let her use the washing machine. I'd have been delighted if she had used the washing machine! Anyway, it was discovered that she was pregnant so naturally I took her back again, for she needed support. For a while she wasn't too bad, she started cleaning and doing stuff around the house. Then the next thing she started her performances again, and I threatened that if she didn't stop messing about I would find a hostel place for her. Another thing: we thought for many years that she was epileptic. Indeed, she was taking medication for epilepsy, and then when she was about 16 – her mother was still living then – we were told that she hadn't got epilepsy. They had done all these tests, and decided that she wasn't having real epileptic seizures, but pseudo-seizures. Yet she'd ended up in hospital a few times. She'd disappear off with friends some weekends, without telling me where she was going. Then you'd get a phone call: 'L____'s in hospital' – she'd taken a turn in Ardoyne or wherever she'd be staying. On one visit to the hospital the doctor said to us: 'Did you notice the marks on her arms?' She had been cutting her wrists – now not deep, it was mostly scratches – and also her legs. And I said: 'Yes, this has happened before and I have spoken to the doctors about it.' This particular doctor said to me 'Do you think she needs help?' And I said 'Of course she needs help, and I have asked for help before, but there has been none forthcoming. So I'm asking you for help again.' Now, I didn't see her for another week because when she got out of hospital she went to stay with a friend. And I don't know what the outcome was. I don't know whether they *did* speak to her, or whether when they eventually offered her counselling she said 'no'. We don't know what happened.

And then she joined Sean's group. I found with Sean's group that she seemed to settle down a terrible lot. I suppose she found people in the same situation as herself and realised that she wasn't this... 'headcase', as she always classed herself. And she would have come and told me what happened in the group. That they were going away for a day somewhere, that they were doing this and doing that. I think it really helped her to settle down. She started going with a boy; she was in a hostel for a while. She's now living in Poleglass in a flat and has about six weeks to go in her pregnancy. But she is a different person now. Don't get me wrong, there's still wee sparks of the old L____ there, but she has really calmed down and can talk to you. I'll give you an example. When we would all go up as a family on Cemetery Sunday to the City Cemetery L____ would say: 'I'm not going.' And I have another two other children, both older than her, and they would go ballistic: 'You *have* to go, your mummy and your sister are both buried up there!' 'I'm not going!' 'Why not!' 'No reason, I'm just not going.' And I would have said: 'Look, leave it, that's the best way.' And just the other day, without anyone asking her, she said: 'I'll be there.' And she was. So she has settled down a great deal. And I'm not worried about her having a baby soon, I think she'll cope fine. In fact, I think it's what she really wants; I think she wanted to be pregnant from she was 16 – to have something that was really hers. She always felt excluded for some reason or other, and she was the youngest of the family. But we never got to the root of her problem.

That last comment echoed another parent's experience.

I don't think you ever get to the root of things. My wee girl was a good child all her life, I never had any problems with her at all. But I think she went from being a child to suddenly being an adult, there was no slow transformation – like going through the whole adolescence thing. She would have been very childlike up until she was about 16 and then she wanted to start growing up – fast. And that's when the problems started. There was one week she wanted to stay over at somebody's house and I said she couldn't, and it ended up she stormed out and went up to her daddy's house – her father and I were separated – and she stayed there. And that was on a Friday night and in the early hours of Sunday morning I got a phone call from her daddy to say she was in the hospital – she had taken an overdose. And as well as being really concerned, I also felt really angry that she had done that. I went up to the hospital and the next day she seen this psychiatrist and they asked was there any reason why she had done it but we got no answers. The week after she got out of the hospital I took her away for a holiday and while we were away two of her friends committed suicide – in fact, there was a third – this was the time there seemed to be a spate of suicides happening in North Belfast. So she was very depressed over all this, and she used to lie in her room all the time. To be honest, I used to hate her lying in her room, because she was always listening to this sad music, sad songs, and I just didn't know what was wrong with her. She was complaining that she could never sleep and just wasn't herself at all. I desperately wanted to know what was on her mind, what she was thinking, because we couldn't get to the bottom of it. More worryingly, I had noticed, before she went into hospital, that some Diazepam – which a relation of mine had left in the house – was missing. And this particular day I came home from work and happened to see her schoolbag sitting there. I know I shouldn't have looked through it, but, to tell you the truth, I wanted to see if there were any of the missing tablets in it. And I found these four letters – one was addressed to her father and three to her [deceased] friends – and they were all suicide notes! And in the letters to her friends she was talking about going to meet them in heaven. I panicked and didn't know what to do. I phoned the doctor and asked her to come over immediately. Now, my daughter was upstairs in her room, and I had actually been afraid to look into the room to see if she was breathing, but I did and thankfully she *was* breathing. And until the doctor arrived I paced up and down the living room, feeling totally, absolutely helpless, couldn't do anything. Anyhow, the doctor finally came and she read the notes and went upstairs. And my daughter looked at me really annoyed, as if to say: what have you done, bringing the doctor out here! When the doctor felt she had to make mention of the notes, she actually said: 'You shouldn't have gone near my schoolbag!' And I says: 'Well, I felt I had to do something.' Afterwards the doctor came down and says she thought that she was sad and very lonely, she was a very unhappy child. The doctor said that she would come out the next day and have a chat with her, which I was delighted with, and then she arranged for us to go to the parents centre on the Lisburn Road.

Well, it was very shortly after that that she joined this programme, and at the start there was about six or seven of them in the core group and I knew that every one of them had tried to self-harm. And I think that really helped her, because it started to bring her out of herself a bit. And I think it's maybe listening to other people's experience, and realising that she wasn't the only one who was like this, that has helped her. And she's been fine up to now; there's no more of the old depression or lying in her room or being tired all the time. I just think, and hope, that it was a phase she was going through in life.

Another parent spoke of her son's circumstances:

When my son was nine months' old his father was put in jail and he was 17 before his dad got out. I had also been to jail. Anyway, the problem all started when he came home from work one day. My son was almost 18 by this time and had got a part-time job as an apprentice chef. He and I were sitting talking while we watched TV that night, but this time his talking seemed a wee bit strange, he didn't sound the same, and, worryingly, he kept going into the bathroom to be sick. He wasn't working the next day so he went to the doctor's, and the doctor said it was like nerves in his stomach, and gave him some medicine. Yet about 4 o'clock that same day I was on the phone to the doctor again. And it was the hardest thing I ever had to do, but I said: 'I think my son is having a nervous breakdown.' All during the previous night he had just wanted to talk and keep talking, and kept going back to his childhood. In fact, his father went out a walk around the town with him, about three or four in the morning. He wanted to talk, and didn't want to be on his own. So, anyway, we went back up to the doctor's and she too felt he was having a breakdown. She gave him Diazepam '5' and '10': three '5's a day – one in the morning, one at lunchtime, one at teatime – and then a '10' at night to get him asleep. And that was for a full week. In the meantime she got in touch with Knockbracken to get him assessed. During that week he seemed to withdraw right into himself, although he still didn't want to be left on his own. But he wanted to talk. If he remembered stealing 10p out of my pocket when he was five he felt he now had to tell me about it. When I was in jail he was actually afraid of me getting out: he always had this thing in his head about Loyalists coming to our house to shot me. I remember my mother looked after him when I was in jail and she said he used to have nightmares about it and worried a lot about it. Anyway, that whole week his father and I took it in turns to sleep on the floor in his room because if he woke up in the middle of the night he didn't want to be on his own. That whole week was like a really bad dream, you didn't know what to do, you couldn't do anything to help him, and these tablets were just like doping him. Then we went to Knockbracken for his assessment. I got a taxi up with him and on the way there I was saying to myself: 'Am I really doing this? I am bringing my son to Purdysburn and I mightn't get him home with me.' He wasn't kept in but was referred to a day centre for counselling and was given a mountain of tablets. That's the only way I can describe it – a mountain of tablets. And he didn't want to go outside the door. When his friends would call to the house – they didn't know what was wrong with him – he would put them off by saying 'I can't go out, I have an ulcer and it's playing me up.' He was very self-conscious about it. Also he was someone who used to love buying clothes, and as he had some money saved up in the credit union we walked round and round the town with him looking at the shops. But he couldn't have cared less: there was just no life in him, no happiness in him, his eyes were dead, that's all I can describe it as. Through the counselling they said it was probably all to do with everything that happened in his childhood: his father being absent all those years and then me being arrested when he was nine and him having to go and live with his granny – it was an unsettled way of life for many years. Anyway, after that first involvement with counselling he took a dive again and we rang to get him another appointment. But they just doubled his tablets – doubled everything he was on. And I sort of lost my head and said 'No, you're not taking them!' He was bad enough with the tablets he was on, he was just sitting there like a cabbage. And they had just double-dosed him! The words I used were: 'Son, you take them and you're going to sit there like Forrest Gump. If you want to do that, that's up to you, but I don't want you to.' We went to our own GP and he halved the dose.

Gradually he sort of decided that he was getting better and started going out with his mates again. But it was a real struggle, he wasn't really ready. I would say he's 75% better, but he still doesn't go out much, and when he does he only stays away for half an hour and then he's back. A couple of years ago he went out one night with a crowd of friends and he came back and just sat at the end of the bed and cried. And he was 22 then. He did want to go out, he did want to be part of the crowd, but he hated it when he was out – he was panicky, he threw up in the toilets, and he just wanted to get home. And when he got home he just sat down and cried, saying: 'I don't fit in anywhere.' And things are still a struggle for him. See if some kid in the street shouts something at him, that will play on his mind. Instead of bantering back and forgetting it he'll keep whatever they said in his head. He'll come in and he'll worry about it, and he thinks he has to tell you. 'Why do you think he said that to me?' He's been everywhere, he's been to counselling, the heap. Now, he's going to a psychotherapist and he's paying privately, £35 a month himself. Because he *wants* to be like everybody else, but it's like trying to get out of a tunnel.

But isn't that better than any tablet – *wanting* to do it? Being motivated.

But what scared me was the amount of tablets they were willing to throw at him.

Mine's was the opposite. Rather than prescribing tablets they suggested only counselling.

It seems to be the luck of the draw, whether you get tablets or something more one-to-one.

Did *any* of the children provide any hint as to what might be at the root of their problems?

They don't really talk about it. And it's such a delicate thing as well, that you don't know how to handle it, you're just afraid. It's as if you're walking on ice and you're afraid of slipping. Because you know they're at that stage where they need your help but you're afraid to say the wrong thing in case they go off the rail.

You're almost afraid to have an argument or disagree.

That's what I went through for a hell of a long time with my daughter. Giving her her own head, and her mother was the same too: 'Okay, go ahead and do what you're going to do.' But it didn't work. So we decided that we would go the other way and really clammed down hard on her. But that didn't work either. There didn't seem to be an explanation for anything that she done and she could never sit down and tell you. There were times she would have talked, and some nights she waited up on me and I would ask: 'What's wrong, are you not going to bed?' And she'd say: 'No, I want to talk.' And so we sat and talked, and I'd have said: 'Now, you have to do this and you're torturing your mother, and you can't carry on like this and giving me a hard time and giving your brother and sister a hard time. They're suffering after losing their sister, you'll have to give everybody a chance.' And there were times when she was quite amenable and saying: 'Daddy, I know that what I'm doing is hurting everybody. And I'm going to stop it.' And that would last for about three days and then just straight back in again – disappear for about two days, you wouldn't have known where she was. And she run about with some of the worst people you could think off, and not only was it embarrassing but it was scary because you didn't know what she was doing, or what other people were doing to her. Because although she is almost 20 she acts younger and is very easily led. She is actually living now with a young fella in Poleglass. And she has now become a better person. She will come and visit us regularly; she is clean, she is tidy and she is eating healthy food. And she's a nice person. We can actually sit and talk to her, she doesn't fight with her brother, she doesn't fight with her sister. I would run her up home at the end of the night, she would stay all day, and get a good-night kiss. And like every father you pray for them every night before you go to bed, hope they're all safe, especially this one because she has always been the troublesome one. But lately I have found myself being more relaxed about it.

What did the parents think was needed to impact upon such problems?

Their group meetings for a start; they are so important to each one of them. I don't know what they would do without that support.

J____ really looks forwards to the meetings. There was a couple of weeks when it was postponed and he really missed it. It's an outlet, outside of the house, where there are people his own age he can talk to.

It's such a simple thing that they need, where they can just meet and explain their feelings to each other – 'This is what I went through' – and it seems to get it off their shoulders. L____ would have come home skipping: 'We had a really good meeting, daddy.' And I would have sat and listened to her talking away: 'Sean says we're going here', and 'Sean says we're going there, and we're going to do this...' That mood could have lasted 3 or 4 days and then she might have gone back again. But then, closer to the weekend or whatever, especially if they were going away, she would have perked up again.

I was really surprised when I first heard that J____ talks a lot at their meetings because it was something he was always very private about. So it must be a very therapeutic thing for a group of people with similar problems to sit and share those problems.

As well as support groups for the young people themselves, I would like to see a parents' support group, and not only for people whose children have gone through self-harming or attempted suicide, but a parents' advice group where they can discuss *any* behaviour that might be worrying them. Even those with 'kids' the age of some of our ones – in their 20s – for many parents have problems with their children no matter what their age is.

Or even an umbrella group, bringing in parents and their children as well.

Yes, just somewhere they could all come along to for a wee chat.

How widespread did they think the problem was?

I think many families are vulnerable but they just don't realise it. Especially families with young men. Many young men today don't see any future for themselves, don't have any sense of self-worth. They're actually living and trying to achieve something they will never get. And because of that they might self-harm or contemplate suicide.

I think the expectations of young people today are unrealistically high, they're not like our own were. When we were young any job would have done, just to bring in money. Your mother and father got you into a job as soon as they could. I think that most young people leave school as quickly as possible, and they think they're going to attain fame and riches very quick and it doesn't happen and will never happen.

They want it now, they want everything now.

I think also we have spoiled them, so it's our fault as well. We didn't have things when we were young, and then when we had children of our own you always tried to give them more than we ever had. I did anyway.

There are different pressures on kids nowadays.

We lived to survive and yet there's kids now don't even want to live. The kids now get all this stuff thrown at them all the time, especially from the TV. The TV constantly feeds them all these unrealistic images of high living, instant fame and possessions. And they feel they need it all and can't do without it.

What should go into the booklet? What should parents do if they have concerns about their child's behaviour?

The first thing to do is to listen to whatever your child is saying, assuming that they're prepared to talk to you. Try to see what the problem is, or how deep it is.

And don't pass judgements on their behaviour while they're talking to you.

And don't belittle their problems. My sisters would have come in and said: 'Well, is L____ acting up again? Well, you know, L____ is L_____' – as if it was just a wee behaviour trait. And that was the answer to everything. And even now if they say that she herself will say: 'No, L____ is *not* L____!'

Just ask them directly: 'Are you worried about something; you don't seem to be yourself lately? Let me know if there's a problem, or tell your mummy or whoever you want to. But don't hold it in.'

The school counsellor should be in the school maybe one or two days a week but the rest of the week he or she should be based outside the school so that visits can be made in a more confidential manner.

The first thing any parent would consider is to take their child to a doctor, but it can often be a hit and miss thing. You might get real sympathetic help or you might just get a load of pills thrown at you.

And doctors scare young people. Especially the word 'psychiatrist'; it just scares them.

My neighbour has a Community Psychiatric Nurse visit twice a week. He didn't want to go to Purdysburn, because apart from being scared that he wouldn't get out again, he felt his neighbours would have known he was going there and treated him like a 'nut'. And the visits really helped; he said it was the best thing every happened to him – just somebody talking to him.

Even when J____ was going to the Day Centre he would have got a taxi from outside the district, rather than use the local one, because people might talk. He'd say to me: 'They know where I'm going.'

There is a real stigma about anything about 'nuts' – and children especially can be very cruel.

People associate suicide with stigma and sometimes it is easier to ignore signs and symptoms because if you start to realise that there are these wee signs or symptoms that your child may be contemplating suicide then there is the worry: what if such-and-such a person finds out? So, it's easier to ignore the signs. But if this booklet shows that other people have gone through all this then maybe it will reassure them.

Psychological problems are so invisible and the mind is a very fragile thing.

I can even see J____ now looking out for his wee brother. He will say: 'We should move, the way the kids around here are growing up now, there's drugs and all...' And you can see him near getting into a panic over it. I say to him: 'But it's everywhere these days.' 'Yes, but out to the country or something, get out of it.' You can see him worrying that all this is in front of his brother and he doesn't want him to go through what he went through.

What about parental guilt?

With me it was definitely there, because I was all he had and then I went to jail. I felt guilty about his whole unsettled way of life. Then his nightmares about the Loyalists coming. Even in the riots of 2003, everybody would have been out at night – I would have been in the community centre helping out. And my big fella would have minded the wee one. But whenever there was a bang he was on the phone, and I gradually had to stop coming round to the centre. I was coming home one night and a neighbour stopped me and said: 'J____ was looking for you earlier. He stopped me and asked: "Did you see my ma?" '... and give her a full description of what I was wearing – 'She's wearing cream jeans and a red jumper and she was round in Clandeboye; do you know what that bang was?' Was he afraid of me being killed? I couldn't put him through all that, even if I was only here in the community centre, so I had to stop coming. A couple of weeks into his breakdown he followed me round the house – this big lump of a fella – and I was putting washing away and he was standing in the landing and he was talking and talking and talking.... And I got down on my knees and just banged my hands on the floor, and says: 'I want my son back that I had before!' And see for a day or two, because he'd never seen me crying, that sort of shocked him: 'My ma's crying! I have to get better.' You don't want to see your child like that.

This woman said to me that she had lived with the guilt for a long time, but there eventually came a time when she realised that there was nothing she could have done, and that she couldn't keep holding herself responsible. Because she *wasn't* responsible: in many cases there was just *no* answer as to why some young people kill themselves. And eventually she came to accept that. So she's always telling others who are constantly blaming themselves that while the sadness of losing a child will never go away, the feeling of guilt will eventually pass.

You could train up parents like her who have been through it, so that they could help and advise others.

A young fella recently knocked my door. A member of his family had been abusing him; he only wanted advice, but he was afraid to go to a solicitor in case it all fell back on him. I just sat and talked to him and put him in touch with somewhere to stay outside the district. But you could see a despair in him too. He had a job, girlfriend, there was good things in his life but he had this sadness, and there was no call for what was happening to him. I listened to him because I would have been glad for someone to listen to *my* son if he had rapped on anyone else's door.

There was mothers on TV last week talking about their children's suicides and thank God we haven't got to that stage. All them sad faces, and broken hearts, and the brothers and sisters, and grandparents. The sooner the funding comes in to help communities tackle this thing the better.

My son'll phone me non-stop. He went to a Celtic match recently – only because his uncle was going as well – and I got at least 15 phone calls: 'We're getting off the bus onto the boat', 'We're getting on the boat', 'I got a fry there and you know how much it was? £9!'; 'We're getting off the boat now, we're on the bus'; 'We're going into the match now, ma'... he has to tell you that he's alright.

But he's also reassuring himself.

I am hoping this booklet will raise a lot more awareness around the whole issue. I hope that when people read this it will help them see that suicide can happen in any family. And that anybody – and I know we are focusing on young people – but anybody who self-harms or tries to take their own life is not somebody from another planet but just an ordinary individual who has got very depressed or sees no light at the end of whatever tunnel they are in. So I'm hoping that it raises more awareness.

Strangely – or perhaps not – one of the parents ended the discussion with sentiments akin to that expressed by the young people:

It's good even talking now.

Are there any lessons?

The alarming increase in incidents of self-harming and suicide – and the trauma visited upon those families directly affected – has engendered deep fears and concerns right across our society. It is imperative not only that we put in place adequate resources to help tackle, and if possible reverse, this trend, but that we begin to identify its possible causes.

With that in mind, what can we draw from the different experiences and views voiced so honestly and openly – by both young people and adults – in this pamphlet? Is it possible to draw up a list of 'guidelines' as to which factors – whether personal or social – are most prevalent in such cases? Or a list of 'indicators' which might provide a warning that all is not well with a loved one? Seemingly not, for it is the consensus that the factors which might precipitate self-destructive actions are not only complex but highly individual. Furthermore, as one of the young people noted, some of what might otherwise pass as 'danger signs' are often, for many adolescents, a normal part of growing up. And if a parent jumps in too quickly it can damage a willingness on the young person's part to share genuine problems later.

Nevertheless, there were some possible causes – boredom, lack of self-esteem, unemployment, drugs, etc. – and some possible indicators – anxiety, hiding in one's room, lack of motivation, etc. – which might be worth keeping very much in mind.

The most frightening aspect is that in many suicide cases there have been no easily identifiable causes or warning signs whatsoever. A woman once told me that she gave her son £5 to get his hair cut barely a hour before he killed himself. She was left totally devastated, for there had been no hint of *any* problems in her son's life. Another woman, who too had lost her child through suicide, now gives talks to concerned groups, and if someone asks her what warning signs they might look out for, she produces a cap-gun from her handbag and fires it point blank at her startled audience, saying: '*That's* the warning you usually get with suicide!'

One thing which both young people and adults were agreed upon, however, was *the need to talk*, to share feelings, problems and fears with one another. In this age of global communication technology it seems ironic to be appealing for us to talk more to one another, but much of what passes for communication these days is often trite or inconsequential. There are admittedly problems regarding communication: young people often feel they cannot discuss things with their parents because of the so-called 'generation gap', and many cannot even tell their friends either, because of concerns about being ridiculed. But talk they must, especially if they are struggling with deep-seated anxieties. And we – parents, relatives, community workers, caring professionals and others – must always make ourselves available to listen.

And if that communication cannot be readily achieved with parents or friends, then self-help support groups are not only vital, but, as is amply revealed by the testimonies in this pamphlet, highly effective and productive. Such support groups can offer amazing results yet require minimal initial funding.

'Space' for this communication to take place is another important consideration. A community worker I know once surveyed a large number of youth groups, trying to ascertain what sort of youth provision the young people wished to see put in place. And while some groups did suggest expensive recreational facilities, the broader consensus was far more simplistic. As one young person put it: 'What we'd really like is a wee hut somewhere, with a couple of sofas in it. Somewhere we can sit and chat with one another.'

In the long term we need to take a serious look at where our society is going, and, more importantly, what we are doing to our children. Formerly, to be classified as 'a young person' was simply an acknowledgement of a developmental stage in life. Nowadays, however, 'young people' are increasingly viewed as commercial targets to whom different interests within the business and entertainment sectors attempt to sell everything from the latest technological gadgets to ever-changing fashions and unrealistic dreams – and in the process the age when childhood seemingly ends is being pushed ever lower. This cannot be wise. Children robbed of a fulfilling childhood will make insecure adults. Likewise, children forced to act like adults before their time will hardly feel able to share still-existent childhood fears with those in the 'grown-up' world.

The very complexity of the problem might put off those who say that nothing much can be done even in the short term. However, small groups such as the SPEAK project in Short Strand show that something can *always* be done, and that in different communities people are beginning to do it – with or without help from government.